Catch a Lover Falling II

Love Poems
by
e. smith sleigh

Other Poetry Collections:

THESE THINGS are a One Thing
OUR NATURE: External Landscapes
THIS NATURE: Internal Landscapes
MUSINGS FROM
THE FAULT LINE AFTER DARK
AN AMERICAN STILL LIFE
VERITY IS RELATIVE: Emma's Memoir
CATCH A LOVER FALLING (Part 1)
JACK
or
In Those Days Jack Henry Claire was Not That Rare

For images, excerpts, a blog, illustrations
and ordering information visit:
http://esmithsleigh.weebly.com/

Artistrie & Associates
2018

… in love's murmur from dusk to dusks
not distant from my still-beating heart

-- e. smith sleigh

love’s conditions

the going and the coming of it
the longing for and the hating of it
the wrong   and the righting
has taken a long while
some toll
there is no easiness
there is no comfort

only the presence or the absence of it

only sometimes, will nurtured love
grow strong and not break
only sometimes does love
endure life’s falls

-- e. smith sleigh

dear

I'm too familiar with this word of
endearment he wrote but there it is

too well used or not used often enough
the word makes me want to kiss him
starting at his brow

too much reward for one word
yet there it is
stalking me in other parts of the house

as I begin to write
the word follows me across the page
and as I fall asleep   I ask

why do I feel so close to him
why do I feel an intimacy with him

I know things about him before he tells them to me
too familiar this relationship in this age of distrust

        I long for him to
                write the word again
                    to
                say the word against my neck

-- e. smith sleigh

full love

my heart is full this morning with nothing in particular
except the love for another human being
the exchange of endearments and ideas
the fire   no doubt   and the wonder of it all

ahhh the purity and excitement of first time lovemaking
visions   feelings and body parts   fantasies

he asked me what I liked
and did it

linger here, no longer there
here we are further down the road than
we thought we could go

you asked me   do we have to remember us
before our hearts overflowed

-- e. smith sleigh

impact

of course   our love resonates throughout my life
I found you irresistible
I discovered profound companionship

you revealed to me a primal, sexual
reaction on every level of my existence

I was transformed   even my body changed
I loved how frequently we had sex
how we fit together
how we talked   and laughed
how sentimental you were

curious   how you cried
when you stared into the sky

-- e. smith sleigh

ohhh,   hey

  you backed me into love
way back into love
backstreet love
alley love
love in the garden
all night steamroller love
wrecking ball love

  come to me now as the dawn rises
and tell me that kind of loving is bad

  you, exhausted lover
you, lover who can't walk straight
sing a hymn to good loving like that
and return to me when the sun goes down
mmmm   love in blacks and grays
and maroon wines   affirmations

  in our nights interminable
we were inexhaustible
our love was boundless

-- e. smith sleigh

inclined to love

how can a kiss encapsulate a life
a kiss faces down weakness and
vulnerability and tells
what can't be told in any other way

after lovemaking, when you hold me
we kiss and
you brush my hair away from my face

in that instant we realize
we are smitten,
not by each other,
but with the intensity of love itself

that’s when you catch a lover falling

-- e. smith sleigh

take it or leave it

at one time   I had no strong feelings about sex, one
way or the other   I often said I'll take it or leave it

it's a phrase that indicates somebody can either
accept or refuse something

when we made love the first time, you took my nipples
and pulled them forward slowly toward your chest
just a little
I shook my head and told myself to take it or leave it

then you twisted them, squeezing them gently
between your thumbs and forefingers until
I screamed   the pain was exquisite

I have no idea how much time passed
but I screamed until I came

'take it or leave it'

you whispered   'you should be able to tolerate a new
situation, especially one involving sex

when I'm around, these things will happen'

-- e. smith sleigh

the assurance he spoke

I want to continually fall in love with you
such pleasure we derive from each other's bodies
and thoughts and actions

we're capable of maintaining oneness without
collapsing or breaking love's connection

I want us to accept adoration without wavering
prepared to accept this prize, this glory

you, dear one, are my regular habit
'it's not too late tonight to take you to bed again'

I hear the music we composed in the background

our love will endure hardship
we will never leave each other
cold and alone

-- e. smith sleigh

let's take a taxi or taxi down the runway or something

we were too far out of town before I realized
we were too far away to return that night

we were too far out into big sky country before I
remembered that you might not want to be there

we were too entangled in each other's bodies to stop

we were too delighted with each other not to respond
to the colors of the sunset
or the moonlight cast into our eyes

we fell too hard to be rescued even though it might
have been a good thing

I wrote a poem on your behind
you wrote a song on mine
we might not have understood the symbolism or
the gravity of the acts

on the third night, before we realized the second night
had passed, you told me you wanted to be there

forever, maybe me you us to be there

-- e. smith sleigh

dawn intones a melody

I sing to my lover

I call to my lover

through a blue and silver dusk
and listen to his reply
as it comes running
through the gold of this morning

he replies by calling my name
then repeats the refrain that I sing

I open my arms wide

-- e. smith sleigh

shoals

after our swim, we were tired, I was wrapped in
a beach towel like your love was wrapped around me

I wanted to sit in the sun, expose my body
to the light   and the still water

I expected my nakedness to work on you, it had an
effect   but in an unintended way   you massaged me
and we fell asleep

we became entangled like the tines of two forks in a
disorderly drawer   but with sunburns

you dreamed this --

earlier, we traveled along the road that ran parallel to
the beach and took the first road on the right   we hit the
dunes in a fast vehicle and almost buried the front end
in a sandbank

dreams are risky   outlays   expenditures
sometimes imaginings can turn real

-- e. smith sleigh

our love at play

no offerings on this sunny day in the paddock
except existence
the sunshine collapses into our molecules
how lovely can this kind of warmth be

at the stables, the trembling colt leapt up when we
approached   we laughed   then comforted him
we petted him until he felt more confident with us

‘did you open your invitation’

“please don’t ignore a future where it’s you
surrounded by love and encouragement   are you going
to tell me something better than that is out there

music --   I’ll help you with your music
when we finish school, we’ll make the decisions
please don’t struggle with whether you can still belong
you are welcomed here

don't flee like a skittish colt
someone who loves you entreats you not to go
don’t go”

-- e. smith sleigh

the song I found

now I dare not sing of love in a little song
or find it in horses' neighs

I found words on the paper that smelled
of a smoky meat locker
and a part of the barn where the herbs
and flowers dry every fall
you wrote of love that carries concern for
the other one in your heart

it said you were too far away to close the distance
between your heart and your lover's heart
or to return from a darkness that picked you up from
the hay-strewn floor and carried you out the door

I read the words on the paper out loud
I was confused by them
then I realized they were the first lyrics you
wrote on your own time   after school ended

I was always afraid that the words would,
would fade away   or stay

where were the predictions for always
later   these words were your first hit

-- e. smith sleigh

taken

i.

don't call me angel   but I did find my love in
the sky   he was always hovering like fireflies on
hot summer evenings

sweat trickled down my back after lovemaking
we ran in the house for something to drink
and pretended nothing happened

ii.

I took you by the arm and steered you out of her way
did she really think she would take first in a competition

she placed you in your chair at the table and leaned over
to feel your chest with both hands,   this was the 15th
take of that scene, she longed to collect something from
you like credit, glory, or shame

she felt she deserved you
that you were something she could win or maintain

for your love, I endured what was unpleasant, the
unavoidable

iii.

we took the first road on the left
stopped taking lunch breaks
and took each other during lunch
we took the Sunday paper then went flying

we moved in with each other
don’t call me a little devil or Maleficent
just call me the dark horse   the victor
but never an angel

-- e. smith sleigh

charm

weekend days full of not much interest
we weren't going anywhere for a while drifting
wrapped in blankets and city views
warmed by faux fireplaces, steaming coffee,
and one another

somewhere someone was playing a bass fiddle
during another brick-building lost-day rehearsal

later in the evening we all piled out of the bar
and into the frozen alley
Sara screamed she wasn't sorry she was pregnant

some timelines intersected here
there once was a strange, enchanted boy
who was mine

the likelihood he'll sing a song for me is 100%
he is the somebody with that voice
he is my other he is my fire on icy days

-- e. smith sleigh

in different coats

singing on the frozen sidewalk tundra   to a
syncopated humming of lights   turned icy blue
in winter   breathing in a wintry wind that locks up our
lungs on a chilled to the bone Wednesday   in the auto
free zone

thinking about drinking frigid vodka

we're searching for some answers about our future
seeking solutions in the bottom of something icy cold
or bubbly hot

we never liked their explanations   perhaps
love   is   just procreation

is   a   is   I believe it's something else   send in the
chill   the black and white photos   the stolen time
loops   the pilfered cases of swill

the juggernauts with nasty knots of not good will

our drinks turn icy blue
we're   breathing in   another winter's wind

-- e. smith sleigh
first published in VERITY IS RELATIVE: Emma's Memoir

don't play a note of the music that could send him away

you said it's sad to think we may not make it
no I said it's too early to end it no way no way

we recalled the day someone played the kind of
music that welcomes love that allows love to move in,
take occupancy

you whispered I know the love I have to give is large
and strong a mighty love a full love an abundant
love a love too valuable to throw away

I agreed

love can be so unkind when every little bit hurts

we played your song loud you hit the piano
'I can't give you all the things you deserve'

I said all I wanted was you
at home right now and not in peril

-- e. smith sleigh

what's your take

in movies a take is a single uninterrupted recording
of a film's action   there may be several takes of a shot,
but only one is used   our life together was like that

a take can be a personal impression or opinion of
something written down   recited   or played

music produced in a single uninterrupted session --
we recorded the song in one take

what's your take on that

we used an old 35mm camera to take a few photos to
record the event

you took musicianship courses and private lessons to
enhance your skills   further your experience
do you mind if I take notes   or write
sometimes you took the bus

and he wanted it that way
in a way, that has nothing to do with taken

-- e. smith sleigh

thunderclouds

thunder crashed through the house
shook the floor under my feet

I waited for you

I saw a crack in the sky
the sky that drew me to you

I heard the announcement of your arrival

you bellowed my name in your sleep
and in the middle of our lovemaking

you were Zeus
I was Europa

I had such a need for you

but I was right not to trust your words
those smooth words that rolled off your tongue
like the purr of a snow leopard

for a while I survived your enticements
you boomed songs around mountain ranges,
cloud formations   and stadiums

after the tour   you summoned me
to your return

-- e. smith sleigh

art of singing

we were the lyrics we wrote

we stumbled over earth so long
we watched for dawn and rain from across the sea
we looked for raindrops and echoes from mountains

we looked for mentions of our music in the papers
we longed for some statement about
                                        our progress online

we traveled in vans and RVs to venues
we waited for aircraft to arrive   then flew our own
we searched for recognition and immortality
we shunned reviews

we staggered over the earth, looking forward to
 anything but love

sometime we were the words we lost

'let's hit the road and find our sex, our love again
it's gotta be daylight somewhere'

we will make another song

-- e. smith sleigh

your decision

you are a lizard in the dunes
no   you are a desert hummingbird
with multi-colored iridescent
silk wings

you see everything: the flowered slopes
the mountain grasses   the turreted buttes

hunting parties
wedding parties

I am a flower
enchant me then

my petals unfurl
your wings flutter
drink me like wine
or a dew drop

-- e. smith sleigh

bridge

conduit

in mid air we were conducted across a chasm
and held aloft by a four inches-thick breadth
of wood shaved from nearby trees

connection

the bridge is tied from one bank   to the other
who threw the rope and missed the opposing cliff
over and over again   who flew through air
or walked across that gorge to build the bridge

who assembled this expanse
bond
link
perhaps it was printer generated

viaduct

I go over   you like under

overpass

railroad bridge near   don't walk that way
run the other
you gamble   I don't

I put my ear to the ground
or the rails   or the planks

suspension bridge

inexpensive bungee cording
for sale:

jumps -- leaps for marriage
you gave the guy the fee he said the words
on our way down
flying gasping
near death but lovingly plummeting

we did it we really did it

-- e. smith sleigh

serenade me

your kiss heightens my senses

enthrall me
arouse me

your touch raises my temperature

caress my trembling body
feel the rhythm of
my simmering passions within

explore all of what I have to give

titillate me
enhance my desire
make me tingle with your soft kisses
and your song

own me
mould me
show me

free me of inhibitions
school me in desire

it's all about you and I becoming one

-- e. smith sleigh

coverings

snow fell in the Algerian desert yesterday
a quarter world away   snow lay on sand
layered granules to layered granules

out my kitchen window here   grey snow clouds
march over the tops of trees   across fields
to plaster an already snow-covered land

I always thought I would walk on top of the layers
of disaffection   survive   and not sink into them

I clothe my feet in snowshoes
my love in an Alaskan parka

steadfast   together
our tomorrows begetting tomorrows
layer   upon layer

-- e. smith sleigh

front man's song

upstairs in my parent's house
I listen to one of our all-time favorites
over and over again
we never got enough of this song

a melody meant for love's interpretation
piecing together of haunting and lovely
a gorgeous accompaniment
laying a track for lovemaking

more divine than divine
it never got any better than that

haunting melody   lyrics   voice
engraving itself in my mind
this song became an addition
a part of our life's soundtrack

-- e. smith sleigh

farewell

he touched my face with leaves of shivering silver from the Aspen grove   he said I have to depart   our music is better than ever   I must be there   I want to be there   with the fans   love me now   I must go soon

his absence became a wound   a sorrow

when I returned to the grove where last we made love
I found a sad beauty   the sting of his absence
and a memory of the soft light in which we lay on the blanket

the soft notes he sang haunt my daylight hours   they feed the hurt and sooth my heart at the same time

where is he right now   I miss him so
I ride through the upland meadows alone to the grove

wonderful melody in the rustling sounds   beautiful light   dancing trees in the evening's mist   the branches touched my face with shimmering leaves

before he left, he whispered in this breathtaking place
"delicate spirit, you satiate all my desires, my need for love"

-- e. smith sleigh

what do you know of her

I wait again
my burdened heart beating with expectation
seeking communication from you
wherever you are

return to me   revisit that sudden revelation
open your eyes to the discovery of the possibilities
of us

I should have pled my case for you to stay
to remain in this warmth,   this desire that fills forests
and yards and rooms

I asked you to linger   and   pass the time with my body
filling your arms   you and me   morphed into a
delicious implement of love   one multi-appendage
organism

one writhing, living thing

-- e. smith sleigh

my visit, sing II

he moved slow, toward the microphone
his feet shifted like a lizard's on hot sand
he surveyed the sea of faces

his mouth opened then he stretched out
a long way he spoke he sung
he owned them with his music
then there were the lyrics
men me the getaway

in the Alps he whispered
'let's have breakfast now
and go skiing later'
what he meant was let's have sex

he missed me
he composed words
from the lack of me
he begged me not to leave
so there would be a
'ain't no where'd ya go'

still, there was something mislaid,
omitted

-- e. smith sleigh
first version published in Catch a Lover Falling

theatre

i.

why didn't you bother to ask *why*
you could have listened to what was inside you
instead of the opinion of everyone around you

you responded
"but it's ...   baby   it's too late"

ii.

I can write these stories
because the stories are about us

gravity pulls at everything on this spinning earth
everything sits on a table
or stands on a platform   or a stage
waiting to roll over the top, fall off the edge
to be used as fuel for a hot, molten core

iii.

it's gravity, it's mechanics
we're tops   turning
spinning   winding down   wobbling
and almost out of time

-- e. smith sleigh

in the gallery

  I much prefer this painting to that one
what is this   it's your mood again

okay we'll go

  how can I hate you, but still love you
you possess no ability to interpret my feelings

  I feel like I'm battling myself in this
mêlée of emotions running through our lives

  this pain originated with you
when you decided to try something new

  what's this you know you can't get a cab here
not after midnight for love or money
you'll have to sit in your car until
the alcohol wears off
you've been so unhappy lately
I won't ask you to stay

  always remember
what you said to me earlier this evening
I was so close to quitting
now I am
all I can say are two words
no more   please get sober

-- e. smith sleigh

count

how many times have you hurt me
I'm supposed to look at you and smile
it's always pleasure obtained by you

who allows *you* to be disloyal

our affair should have been love-uninterrupted
you spent too many days and nights away
my love was true   I was here waiting

it isn't okay to tell me that our love wasn't
that way for you

-- e. smith sleigh

last look around

I was told one day I would welcome
the hug of a teddy bear
how hard your absence has hit my heart

your voice so warm and sensual
echoes around here   I can hear us making love

I gave you all the love I could give
but what did you want in return ...

when you begin your night, tonight
think about our good times

I'll just take another look around
I'll take one of your shirts in the closet
because it smells like you
and I'll take Teddy from the bed
well   I'll go now   but if you ever want to hear my …

no   please   I   mean
I'm alone with my thoughts just talking
that's all   I won't come back
once I go   I'll never look back
never   look ba, bah …

I won't come   around

-- e. smith sleigh

leopard

before this loneliness that you've given me
walked down the highway, climbed into my car
and sat there with me

we shared an uncomplicated love

it waited to be discovered
through our friendship
I kissed your forehead, it ended on your lips
three days later we were us

the radio is on   it's all bass
ooh, stars lead me back home
yes, that *had* to be our song playing

for a long time
 you played at no-love

when you left that last night   you weren't going
to look back   but you did

I caught you   still falling

-- e. smith sleigh

love's home

she no longer imagined their relationship
    as a desert garden filled with
    hummingbirds

their love no longer hovered and hummed
within her chest
    her ribcage was not its
    dwelling

she felt their emotions transmuted
    into a shadowy place
    away from their hearts

as time passed   he phoned several times
to say he was clean and he missed her
she realized their love was not spent

they decided   they were capable of reviving
    their love and devotion

-- e. smith sleigh

une célébration de l'amour

i

say you didn't mean it
say there's love yet again or
that love lingers still

we walk through this night of life
in search of a sunrise
but we are not confident in our search
or that we will discover
the light of dawn once more

ii

be still dear heart and permit the sun to
brush your face
allow my kiss to touch
your cheek and lips once more

permit our love to reside in a timeless
fountain to draw upon again and again
let's restore our love and make it as fresh as
the first day we discovered it

-- e. smith sleigh

vision

solitude
it softened my heart and soul

your music chided me
I truly loved you
we shouldn't have let go

we both longed for sweet tenderness
that overwhelming desire

forgiveness
is the hardest thing for the heart
and soul

in the evening sky
when the half moon rose
we reunited   by the fire
on that cold mountain night

-- e. smith sleigh

there's nothing rational about love

after a renewal of our vows he wandered
off somewhere in the world to sell his
notes to humanity one last time

the songs took a long while
to complete   rehearse   and perform
the show grew more popular as he went
his tour was extended
what usually took several months
took longer

I understood his dream
took time to play out

I tried to meet him in different locations
when we both had time
our love was an outflow   an offering
again our love became the lyrics in his songs

he said he learned from existence that
there was nothing rational about life or love
I went home and passed the time
in anticipation of his return

-- e. smith sleigh

maps

all the magic of our dream-filled life
did not vanish   we fell in love once more
now I'm living the reality of his absences again
his life continues way across the country

I whispered come to me   come to me
we cried together on the phone
I could hear the sound of his tires hitting
the gaps in the pavement on the way to the airstrip

I counted the minutes
our friends said try to hang on

within the same thoughts and words that said I love
you   at the same time , I lost him once again, I don't
want to cry   I just want him and his love that was almost
all mine, through the times that were so hard, that
separated us, all I ever said was come to me
come home to me safe and sound

our friends gathered at the house and said
you'll have to go on

beloved   you were my greatest love
our love was so profound

-- e. smith sleigh

chanson luxe

early spring arrives   someone dies
emotions concealed and avalanching
images carefully curated

still feels like there's something missing
his was a voided world
no matter how short
it was once a life that could brighten skies

where I dwell   the daylight hours
are grey   then sunny   then grey again
these days my eyes crave the sunny morns

to think about what's happened
what is changing   how pivotal forces impact life
feels like   more than just a series of events
small forces crash days
large forces crush life

somewhere there's a sun
of deeper circumstance

la chanson luxe

-- e. smith sleigh
first published in Verity is Relative

specter

I allowed the lemon to waste away in the refrigerator
when I could have used it for my tea but I squandered
its existence and its purpose
I rarely confess such things

hear the roaring

why does this bother me in this hologram of a week
on this night of winds after the turn of a year
such an in-between time   projected subzero dead zone

I hear his voice calling Belov*ed* from far away
how do I respond to my phantasm

-- e. smith sleigh

infernal night

night rises in me like a shadow beast

night rises cascades down my body
like a black silk gown
night rises within the course of my sorrow
night rises through me like Psyche in
the monochrome void
the eddying gulf
the yawning chasm
night buries itself in me
like loss
lost love
lost children
like the damned in their torment
night calls forth in me the lament
the yowl down the stairs
along the unpaved path
through the garden of weeds
up the brackish river
night wallows on me
like remembrances
of an always lover

-- e. smith sleigh
first version published in Catch a Lover Falling

phantom

I've lost love before
but I
like rain
like leaves
like snow
like sleet
like hail

like ice
like angels
like lovers

kept falling

-- e. smith sleigh

take off

my lover   the front man   the pilot
thought he rebuffed death   but he didn't

when I entered the room, a newly extinguished candle,
or was it the people, had sucked away most of the
oxygen   the remaining air was warm   stale

carnations, their scent overwhelming, lolled in strange
vessels

the casket flew out the hanger door

I was supposed to be brave   I was never going to be,
I tried, but I was tired   so tired

on the way home   I looked skyward
I spotted red fireballs cast from the firmament
                                        melting along the horizon
night or day, the sky always made me wonder

looking for him   looking for him

I climb into the blue
nothing is permanent

-- e. smith sleigh

at four a shift occurs

a quiet   gentle stillness
slips into the room
possesses me and the music
lulls me   lifts my spirit
with grace and renewal
resides here until dawn

its resurfacing of
my part of the world
lends existence a new face
gilds the ugly haze
serenades me with a fresh wind
and brightening skies

I'm caught in the magic
I listen closely for a sign

all I hear is a whisper
dance   dance
just
dance

-- e. smith sleigh

nowhere to be found

I'll throw poetry into the sky
and bellow I'll remember

still

I'm losing time
and skylines …

I don't expect an ending

-- e. smith sleigh

Poem List

page

Made in the USA
Columbia, SC
01 September 2020

17987404R00031